Shafted! Everything You Ever Need To Know about the Engine of the Golf Club

I0159261

Doug Gelbert

CRUDEN BAY BOOKS

SHAFTED! EVERYTHING YOU EVER NEED TO KNOW
ABOUT THE ENGINE OF THE GOLF CLUB

Cruden Bay Books
184 Kanuga Heights Lane
Hendersonville NC 28739

ISBN - 978-1-935771-31-9

Shafted! Everything You Ever Need To Know about the Engine of the Golf Club

Introduction

Do you know how golf began? No? You're not alone - no one does. Make up any story you like. Dutchmen banging balls across frozen canals. Lonely shepherds whacking pebbles up and down Scottish sand dunes. Ancient Romans slugging stuffed leather balls towards Corinthian columns. Take your pick. But every origin story you land on has one thing in common - the game is played with a stick.

Today that stick is called a shaft. It is the most important element of the golf club - the only means of imparting energy to the golf ball. The shaft is responsible for the accuracy, distance and trajectory of every golf shot. It is not for nothing that the shaft is called the "engine of the golf club." Like a stock car, you can make all the modifications you want but the best engine is still the favorite to win the race. And the only way to squeeze every last drop of potential from your golf clubs is to have them outfitted with the proper shaft. And yet for most golfers the shaft is the least understood element in golf...

Early kolf players on ice.

History of the Golf Shaft

The year was 1457 and the Scots were digging this new game of golf. So much so that many sportsmen were neglecting their archery practice - a sport that was critical to defending the country's borders. So King James II of Scotland, then 27 years old and known as "James of the Fiery Face" because of a birthmark, banned the game. Or in his official words: "golfe be utterly cryed down and not to be used." He was blown up by one of his own cannons two years later but his son, James III, reaffirmed the ban in 1471. That James was stabbed to death in 1488 by a "mysterious figure" who may or may not have been an aggrieved linkster.

His son, James IV, was only 15 years old but quickly grabbed the reins of power. And in 1491 he, too, reaffirmed the abolishment of golf in Scotland. But sometime while he was jockeying for control over the kingdom with the English James caught the golf bug and lifted the ban on the game in 1500. Two years later he made what is believed to be the first golf purchase. Since there was no eBay or Amazon or golf pro shop James went to an archery bow-maker and ordered a new set of clubs.

King James IV is believed to have been the first to have purchased a set of golf clubs.

For the next 400 years golf shafts would be made out of wood. European hardwoods such as holly and pear and apple were popular for clubheads. At first any hardwood that was available locally and workable was

used for shafts. The King's first clubs were apparently fashioned from Scottish beech. But as sea trade flourished in the 1600s and 1700s exotic woods like danga wood, purpleheart, bulletwood and bloomahoo were tried as golf shafts. After the United States blustered its way into existence in the late 18th century stylish English golfers could be found sporting clubs turned from ash, hazel and lancewood.

The Rise of the Clubmaker

About this time the craft of clubmaking began to drift permanently away from the local bowyer and towards dedicated golf club craftsmen. No longer would golf clubs be dismissed as "rude and clumsy bludgeons" in the hands of undiscerning linksters.

James McEwan was a joiner and cartwright before opening a shop in Edinburgh in 1770 to make clubs for The Bruntsfield Links Golfing Society that had formed nine years earlier as the world's fourth golf club. James was followed into the business

Six generations of McEwans turned out the finest clubs in Edinburgh.

by Peter and Douglas and three more Peters - six generations of McEwans for 127 years signed their name beneath the company's thistle mark logo. Ash was the wood of choice for shafts crafted by the early McEwans.

Hugh Philp was sometimes called the "Stradivarius of Golf" for the balance he was able to achieve with his wooden-shafted clubs. Philp was born in 1786 in Cameron Bridge, best known to-day for the Haig family whisky distillery. He migrated to St. Andrews in his twenties to work as a joiner and housepainter and was regarded around the college town

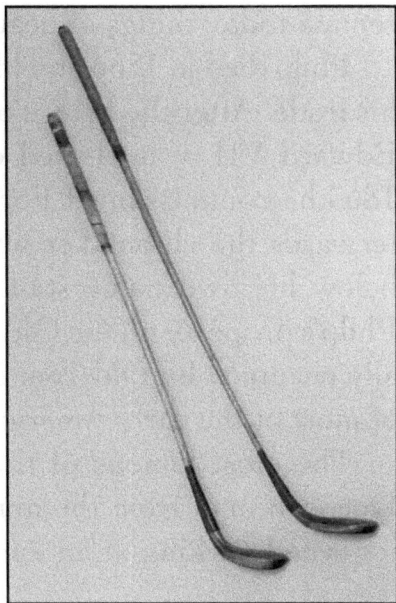

These wooden-shafted Hugh Philp-designed long nosed clubs were the best available 19th century sticks for golfers.

as "a dry haired man, rather gruff to strangers" but possessing a caustic wit he saved for friends. Beyond a line in the poem, "The First Hole at St. Andrews on a Crowded Day," - Here, Mr. Philp, clubmaker is as great a Philip as any Minister of State - little is known of the master craftsman.

Philp took up clubmaking as a sideline in 1812 and in 1819 he was appointed "clubmaker to the Society" of the Royal and Ancient Golf Club. Philp ran the only golf shop in St. Andrews and there was a brisk trade in counterfeit "H. Philp" stamps on his trademark long-nosed spoons and baffies. As *Harper's Weekly* gushed in 1897, "It was Hugh Philp who first departed from the primitive models of the stone age and began to make golf clubs that looked as though they were intended for some gentler work than the crushing in of an enemy's skull or the manufacture of broken flint for road-building. Philp had an eye for graceful lines and curves, and his slim, elegant models remain today things of beauty."

Philp died in 1856 and his nephew, Robert Forgan, assumed his trade. After the Prince of Wales, eventually to become King Edward VII, was elected captain of the Royal & Ancient in 1863 he commissioned Forgan to create a set of clubs and afterwards the clubmaker was permitted to add the royal crest below his own name stamp which jumpstarted his business. Philp's property on the Old Course at St. Andrews was eventually occupied by Old Tom Morris, who became the progenitor of most of the early American golf pros.

The most famous of these was Donald Ross. Ross was a Dornoch man from the north of Scotland who showed a flair for woodworking at an early age. This being Scotland young Donald was steered away from cabinetry and packed off to St. Andrews where his skills could be better applied - making golf clubs under Old Tom Morris. What were these old clubmakers looking for in a wooden golf shaft?

Donald Ross is most famous as a golf architect but he began his career turning wooden golf shafts.

Well, durability for one. Master clubmakers would search for the finest grained wood that could stand up to hard play. And just like today, wooden shafts were valued for their performance, weight and feel. Consistency throughout the bag was also critical. And in the mid-1800s the eternal search for the best wood to turn into golf shafts came to an end.

The revelation came from shipments of axe handles to Britain from the United States. The wood used for these tools was hickory. As grizzled arborists are wont to say, "There are woods that are stronger than hickory and woods that are harder, but no other commercial wood can match the combination of strength, toughness and hardness of hickory." For golf shafts this meant durability without too much weight and power - delivering flexibility without excessive torque. By the 1890s when golfers referred to their wooden shafts, they were talking exclusively about their hickory shafts.

Age of Steel

Golfers were not oblivious to the possibilities of steel as a shaft material. In 1894 master blacksmith Thomas Horsburgh, a top-notch curler as well as a crack golfer at the Baberton Golf Club, fired a set of steel-shafted clubs at his Cockburn Smiddy on Glenbrook Road in Balerno, near Edinburgh. On May 1 he was granted UK Patent No 8603 for "the use of steel shafts for golf clubs for the purpose of giving strength and elasticity." While Horsburgh forged a complete set of woods and irons his true purpose was to create a single shaft into which any clubhead could be screwed on to form a club. During his rounds at Baberton he carried around his single shaft and his trusty henchman lugged along a canvas satchel stuffed with the

Thomas Horsburgh is the father of steel golf shafts.

various clubheads.

Alas, Horsburgh's steel shaft was a solid piece of metal and required the forearms of a blacksmith to swing. The result was that although he whittled his handicap down to a plus-4 and took the Baberton scratch medal several times, Horsburgh allowed his patent to expire in the 1920s as solid steel shafts were not adopted en masse by golfers.

In the US of A, Arthur Franklin Knight was fiddling with steel shafts. His was not a new name to the lords of golf, although for some reason the name he was called was "Bill." Knight was born in Rensselaer, New York in 1868 and grew up to be an electrical engineer for General Electric in Schenectady. He was also an enthusiastic golfer at the local Mohawk Golf Club - and like thousands before him and millions since Knight suffered greatly on the greens. His solution was a blocky aluminum head with the hickory shaft inserted near the center.

Arthur Franklin Knight was an engineer who channeled his energies into golf club design.

Walter Travis, the first American superstar golfer, got a hold of Knight's so-called "Schenectady Putter" and declared it "the best putter I have ever used." He then took one with him across the Atlantic Ocean in 1904 and became the first non-British golfer to win the British Amateur. Six years later the Royal & Ancient outlawed all "mallet-headed" clubs of which the Schenectady Putter was the leading breed. The United States Golf

Association chose to ban only actual mallets - it was the first time the two ruling bodies of golf ever parted ways on the rules.

In 1909 Knight was back at the drawing board, this time with an invention of a "new and useful improvement" to the golf club - a shaft of steel tubing. As Knight described it in his application to the patent office: "In golf clubs as usually constructed the head of the club is secured to a wooden shaft usually of a highly elastic wood such as selected seasoned hickory tapering to a comparatively small section at the head and much stouter at the handle end. Hickory has uniformly been preferred on account of its hardness, toughness and suppleness, the latter quality being very important in controlling the rebound of the head after the powerful impact with the ball and adding to the distance of the drive. I have discovered, however, that with a hickory shaft there is an inherent objection, namely, the Wood being fibrous in nature offers but small resistance to torsional strain and it therefore results that when the blow is delivered to

A.F. Knight's Schenectady Putter scared the sense out of the Royal & Ancient.

11

the ball, the head of the club yields in a line circumferential to the axis, that is to say, the blow being delivered at a point several inches eccentric to the axis of the shaft produces a strong torsional strain which twists the hickory and this effect is accentuated by the nature of the wood, which being in effect a bundle of parallel fibers is easily twisted on its axis. Therefore, when the blow is delivered the head takes a resultant line of motion, one component tending to twist the shaft on the axis and the other to flex it backward. The latter only is the one desired, since a rebound in the direction of the blow would serve only to raise-the trajectory of the balls flight and increase the length of the drive. The torsional element, however, is highly objectionable since an angular rebound causes the ball to deviate from the direction of impact and therefore the direction of aim and the flight will be at an angle to that intended, so that unless the player by long training and practice unconsciously through experience has acquired a standing position to offset this inherent fault of the club, his play will be uncertain and irregular."

He goes on much longer but essentially Knight is saying that hickory shafts are hard to play with. In 1910 he received US Patent Number 976267A. This time, however both the R&A and the USGA agreed - steel shafts with their resistance to twisting in the golf swing would be banned from sanctioned competition. Knight was never quite able to make his hollow

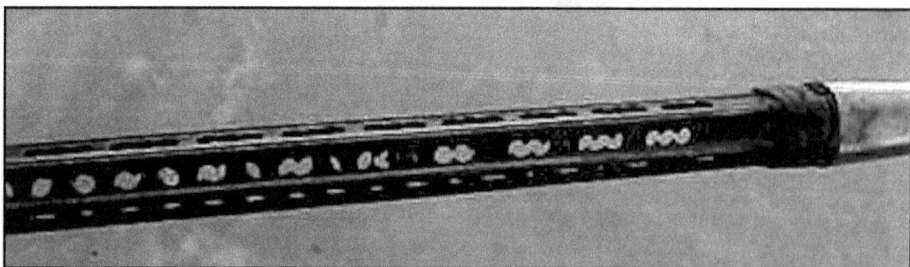

Allan Lard's solution to the heaviness of steel was to perforate the shaft.
The holes caused the club to whistle during the swing, hence the "Lard Whistler."

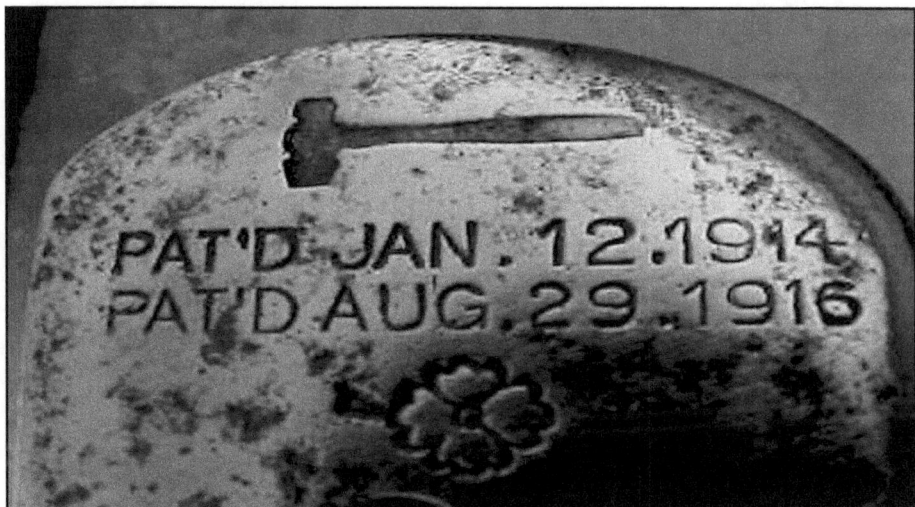

A.G. Spalding acquired Lard's patents for its first steel-shafted golf clubs - marketed under the Uncommon Gold brand.

tube walls thin enough to be practical anyway and in 1920 he sold his patent to the Horton Manufacturing Company. After this, Knight got out of the golf club invention business. He designed a couple of courses around Schenectady and invented a table-top golf game played with tiddlywinks - no hickory or steel shafts necessary.

Steel shafts were still in play for recreational golfers, however, although there was still the matter of weight. The most notable solution came from Allan Edward Lard, born in America's heartland in the 1860s. He played golf in the Olympics in his his native Missouri at Glen Echo Country Club in 1904 and shot 183 for his two rounds to barely qualify for the 32-man match play competition. Lard won his opening match 10 & 9 but was ousted in the next round by Francis Newton 2 & 1. Lard went on to capture the prestigious North and South Amateur title at Pinehurst in both 1907 and 1908.

By this time Lard was also a celebrated inventor for designing a single trigger mechanism for double barrel drop down shotguns. He made many refinements for his trigger before turning his creative mind to golf shaft design. Lard came up with a hexagonal steel shaft with perforations throughout to decrease the weight. During the swing the holes often produced a whistling sound, hence the "Lard Whistler." Allan Lard assigned his 1914 patent to The Metallic Shaft Company of Wilmington, Delaware which produced the steel-shafted clubs for A.G. Spalding sporting goods company which sold them under the Uncommon Gold Medal brand. The "Whistler" was not a success but Lard was already moving on and invented a machine in 1920 to sort and count paper money.

The Age of Steel Truly Arrives

In 1921 the Horton company took Knight's steel tube and heat treated it with a hydrogen brazing process to create a tapered end that enabled the production of a matched set of clubs - slaying the bugaboo that had long afflicted hand-milled hickory shafted clubs. Horton signed on the Crawford, MacGregor & Candy Company as its first customer. And then Wilson and Hillerich and Bradsby (the Louisville Slugger people) and

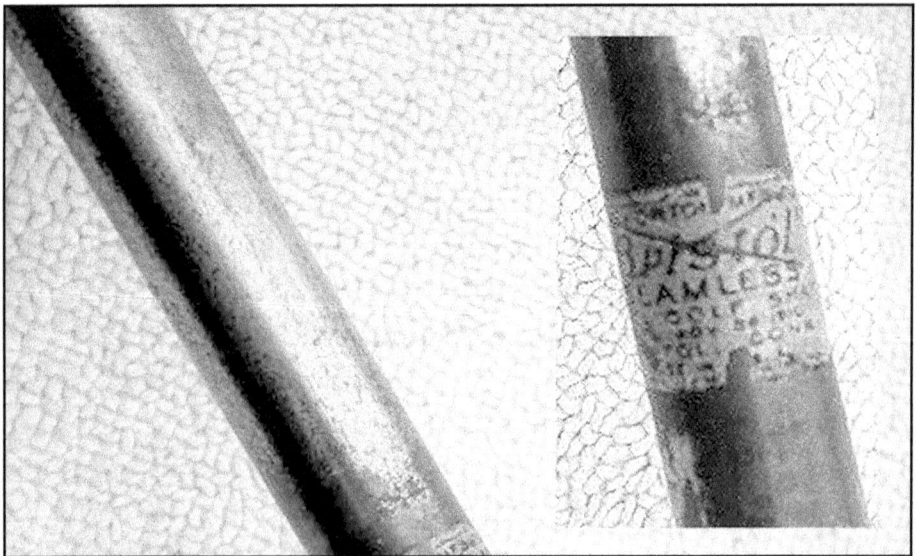

The "Bristol" was the first steel shaft to appear in the U.S. Open.

Spalding all came calling. Horton called its club the "Bristol."

In 1923 the Western Open, staged by the Western Golf Association and ranking just behind the U.S. Open and PGA Championship in importance for the professionals, approved steel shafts for play. Horton representative Herbert C. Lagerblade took the weapons into battle for the first time at Colonial Country Club in Cordova, Tennessee outside of Memphis. As Mr. Lagerblade modestly recounted, his performance "certainly didn't aid my game enough to have me scoring among the leaders."

Horton advertised in the *Saturday Evening Post* to give away a steel-shafted club to any golfer scoring an attested hole-in-one. They sent away more than 700 new Bristols. Then, after a spirited letter campaign to the USGA, America's ruling body for golf, relented on allowing steel shafts in competition. In 1924, at Oakland Hills Country Club in Michigan, Lagerblade became the first golfer to swing steel-shafted clubs in the United States Open championship. In 1929 the Royal and Ancient Golf Club got on board and declared steel shafts legal for tournament play throughout the golfing world.

The conquest of wooden shafts, entrenched for over 400 years, was not complete, however. Bobby Jones still used hickory shafts to win the Grand Slam in 1930 and when Spalding put out its

Bobby Jones won the Grand Slam in 1930 using wooden shafts when steel was legal.

George Von Elm made the last stand against steel shafts.

steel-shafted Bobby Jones signature irons that year the tubes were painted tan to simulate hickory so as not to shatter the delicate nerves of hidebound traditionalists. In 1931 the more than 400-year reign of wooden golf shafts came to an end. But it required quite a struggle. The U.S. Open was at the Inverness Club in Toledo, Ohio that year and with the retired Jones looking on in the gallery the field of contenders was whittled down to two: George Von Elm, a lanky, stylish linkster from Utah and 29-year old William "Billy" Burke. Willie Burkauskas grew up in the Connecticut caddie yards and worked as a puddler in a local foundry where he lost the ring finger and mangled the pinky on his left hand in an accident.

Von Elm set The Inverness course record with a 69 in the second round but could not shake Burke. After 72 holes both players were tied for the lead with a score of 292. In those days that called for a 36-hole playoff the following day. Burke twice forged leads of four strokes during the playoff but both times Von Elm stormed back, once by making four consecutive birdies. So it was 36 more holes. As the *New York Times* reported on the goings-on in Ohio: "The long-waged wars of ancient times have nothing on the wars that two linksmen are now waging in the national open championship."

Back to Inverness for the third consecutive day of 36 holes.

Wags in the sporting press counted Von Elm's cigarettes to calm his nerves and Burke's cigars. The final tote for the stogies was 32. Burke made a birdie from the rough on 143rd hole (#17) to take a two-stroke lead and held on for the win after eight tours of Inverness, 589 to 590. His $1,000 first prize worked out to $125 a round. And he had used steel shafts, whose durability was much-needed in the Open marathon.

Future U.S. Opens would see plenty of steel shafts as hickory players were gone within a few years. But the U.S. Open would see no more 36-hole playoffs. Eighteen holes and sudden-death was deemed sufficient to identify the national champion golfer.

Back in 1902 seventeen tool-making firms combined to form American Fork & Hoe with manufacturing plants in Geneva and Ashtabula, Ohio. By 1930, with continued mergers, 90% of all hand tools used by U.S. farmers were churned out in these factories. There was considerably less land to farm at that point after the first golf course building boom in America in the 1920s. But American Fork and Hoe was still very much a presence on the land in 1929 as the company introduced a steel tapered step-down shaft that permitted different shaft

America's leading tool company became the leading manufacturer of steel golf shafts.

flexes for each golfer.

American Fork and Hoe would change its name in 1949 to True Temper by which time it was dominating the golf shaft market. Things were not going so well in the hand tool trade. Two True Temper executives were convicted of fixing hand-tool prices and tossed into prison - the first corporate jailbirds in American history. But that is a tale for a different chronicle.

By the end of the 1930s hickory shafts had pretty much vanished. The first real consequence to golfers was that the powers-that-be enacted a 14-club limit since the worry that wooden clubs might break during the round was gone. Until that point, golfers could play with as many clubs as their caddies could carry. In the 1927 United States Amateur Bobby Jones used 22 clubs to down Chick Evans 8 and 7. Evans, the first player to win both the U.S. Open and U.S. Amateur in the same year, used only seven. Evans groused that Jones had developed his game "with clubs and not his skull."

Lawson Little puzzled over 31 clubs in taking the British Amateur in 1934. But that was all laid to rest in 1938 with the 14-club carry limit. Why 14? Why is that the magic number? Golf historians believe it was to benefit caddies who commonly did a loop double-bagging for just one golfer.

Space Age Technology

Unlike wood, steel would not have to wait centuries for its dominance as a golf shaft material to be challenged. The first material to emerge from the tireless experimentation during World War II was heat-hardened polyester resin reinforced with high-strength glass fibers - fiberglass. Fiberglass was used in all sorts of structural aircraft parts, including helicopter blades. After the war the first manufacturer to seize on the commercial potential of fiberglass was the Shakespeare Company.

The Shakespeare Fiberglas WonderShaft
came along to challenge steel after World War II.

In the 1890s William Shakespeare, Jr. was a peddler of magical elixirs around Kalamazoo, Michigan. He would often set aside his traveling case of snake oil to drop a fishing line in one of the bountiful bodies of water in the Wolverine State. Shakespeare was continually frustrated with the inefficient reels of the day so he cobbled together his own "level-wind" reel and one of sportfishing's great companies was born. In 1946 Shakespeare brought out the revolutionary Wonderod, a fiberglass fishing pole that immediately sent bamboo and steel rods to the boneyard.

That was quickly followed by the Shakespeare Fiberglas WonderShaft, marking the company's initial foray into golf. More than a half-million glass fibers were bonded into a double-built tubular shaft with the fibers running lengthwise down the shaft and around a central fiberglass wall. Shakespeare touted the "cushiony feel" of its shafts and also trotted out scientific evidence that the shafts absorbed energy and caused less twisting of the club during the swing than steel - the same case steel had made against hickory.

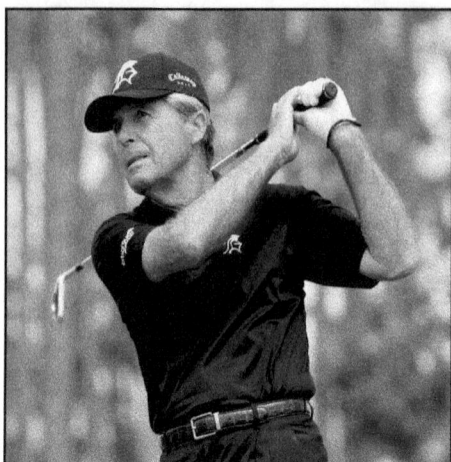

When Gary Player won the U.S. Open in 1965 with fiberglass shafts the future seemed bright for the new technology.

By the 1960s Shakespeare had recruited Gary Player who won the 1965 U.S. Open at Bellerive Country Club west of St. Louis with WonderShafts through the bag. "I think you can stay with the ball longer with Fiberglas, which is very important. The longer you stay with the ball, the better you hit it and the better you control it," he said. Fiberglass is stronger than steel but also heavier and not many weekend golfers had the hand strength of the Black Knight. Fiberglass never caught on in the marketplace.

If fiberglass was too heavy, well how about aluminum? Alum was known in ancient times but it was not until the 19th century that fabricating of the metal was made possible through advances in electricity and chemistry. With the advent of aviation the use of lightweight aluminum became widespread. One such aerospace company was a small manufacturing concern in Santa Fe Springs, California called LeFiell Manufacturing. LeFiell aluminum products have been used in every NASA space mission and Lunar Module parts fabricated by LeFiell still reside on the moon.

In the middle of the 20th century a division of the company called LeFiell Sport was created to manufacture aluminum boat masts, ski poles, pool cues and…golf shafts. Aluminum shafts were lighter than steel and that meant that clubs could be swung faster with less effort to generate more clubhead speed. Physics tells us that will make the ball go further. It is just simple science. Oh yes, and aluminum shafts will not twist as much as steel shafts - the Holy Grail of golf shafts.

In 1967 LeFiell teamed up with the Arnold Palmer Company. On the PGA Tour Arnie dusted the field in both the Los Angeles Open and the Tucson Open with aluminum shafts before the snow had melted in the Midwest. Robbie Robinson, vice president of the Arnold Palmer Company chortled, "This shaft could become the greatest contribution to the golf industry since the introduction of the steel shaft, and it could be a tremendous boon to golfers."

Arnold Palmer found great success with aluminum shafts but it was a brief romance for the space-age material.

Whoa, not so fast, Mr. Robinson. To achieve the same strength as steel aluminum shafts needed thicker walls and as much as golfers crave extra distance they want to look good doing it and those "fat" aluminum shafts were not appealing to the eye. And come cold weather the aluminum shafts had a nasty habit of snapping at impact in the middle of a round. In the final analysis golfers just did not find enough extra yardage in aluminum to give up their steel shafts. The iron-carbon alloy had fended off another competitor.

The Final Word on Shaft Materials?

While Shakespeare was winding filaments of fiberglass into golf shafts Union Carbide was twirling fibers of graphite into lightweight aircraft components for NASA. When Union Carbide sought to crack the consumer market they contacted Frank Thomas who was running the golf shaft show at Shakespeare. The result was the first graphite shaft in 1968, which was introduced to the golf world at the PGA Merchandise Show in 1970.

Graphite is 14 times stronger than steel which meant that a graphite shaft could be constructed that weighed a smidge over two ounces - lighter than aluminum and half the weight of steel. Even more clubhead speed with the same effort! Five more yards! But the cost for that 15 feet was steep; a pound of graphite cost $500, a pound of steel about seven cents. The durability of the fledgling graphite shafts was a problem as well and so was inconsistent performance. Steel trundled merrily along as the dominant shaft material even after the introduction of graphite.

Lightweight titanium made a run at steel in the 1990s but it proved too expensive to be a viable everyday alternative. But unlike rivals fiberglass and aluminum, graphite stuck around and improved with the addition of materials such as boron and Kevlar and steel fibers. As golf plays through the 21st century what should golfers look at when considering the selection of golf shafts?

Choosing Among Today's Shafts

These days steel and graphite shafts live together in most golf bags: where speed and power are the desired result - in the driver and other fairway metals - graphite is used almost exclusively. Where control and feel are the desired result - with the irons - steel is the shaft most often used.

There is no "vice-versa" with the long clubs but graphite is making inroads against steel as shafts for irons. Broadly, you should consider graphite shafts for iron clubs if:

- you want extra distance and are not as concerned about accuracy
- you play with a naturally slow swing tempo
- you have sustained an injury that compromises your ability to swing heavier steel clubs
- you want an increased dampening effect to eliminate the sharp pangs of vibrations from mis-hit approach shots
- this is your last club purchase and you are anticipating a decline in physical ability as you age

Composite carbon fiber shafts are ever improving and are approaching the rigidity of steel every year. Until that time, seek out steel shafts for irons when:

- your swing speed is fast enough to control the golf ball with heavier clubs
- you want to minimize swing flaws caused by excessive whippiness experience with graphite
- you value feedback from mis-hits
- your golfing budget does not have room for expensive high-tech graphite shafts.

What about wood?

As the race for greater technological advantages speeds ever faster along some golfers have stepped off the treadmill and embraced the hickory shafts left in the woodshed over eight decades ago. Many have joined the Society of Hickory Golfers to play tournaments using the classic equipment. Playsets are cobbled together from online sources, garage sales and swap meets.

Enough players have restocked their bags with hickory-shafted clubs that two American companies have emerged to create replica clubs using the same techniques employed a century ago. Louisville Golf and Tad Moore base their club designs on authentic clubs used in the pre-1935 hickory era. Each are approved for hickory tournament play.

Shaft Length

The longer the shaft of the golf club, the further the ball will fly. That is simply sun-rises-in-the-east science. A wide swing base and all that. Master blasters in long-drive competitions used to brandish missile launchers that ranged from 52 inches up to five feet long. Those events have been relegated to You-Tube and the maximum allowable length for regular play is 48 inches. Long-drive contests have fallen in line and adopted the 48-inch maximum.

So the longest legal shaft for a driver will be 48 inches long, as laid out in the Rules of Golf. But the longer the shaft, the more difficult it is to make consistent contact that will reap maximum benefit of those 48 inches. For that reason the standard length for a driver has been between 43 and 45 inches. Thanks to its lighter weight, graphite shafts have stretched driver shafts out an inch to the 45-46 inch range.

Tiger Woods used a relatively skimpy 43.5-inch long driver most of his career. Phil Mickelson has been known to carry two drivers in his bag, including a 46-inch model he pulls out when he needs an extra 20 yards off the tee. The only way to find out the ideal driver length for you is to experiment to find the ideal potion of control and distance. Mixed into that stew will be such ingredients as skill, strength and tempo. Use impact tape to find what driver length provides the most consistent contact since balls struck on the screws with a shorter driver will fly over the off-center hits of a longer one.

Shaft Flex

While the importance of shaft length is obvious shaft flex is more like sleep: everyone knows it is important but not so many know why. The bend in the shaft as the club is swung is known as "flex." The amount of flex during the swing determines how much the clubhead shifts in the backswing and again in the downswing. The more the club flexes the more difficult it is to return the clubhead squarely to the ball to produce the best golf shots.

If you need a rule, the faster the club swings the more it flexes. And the more resistance is required to keep if from flexing - the shaft's stiffness. Hickory shafts flexed a great deal which required immaculate timing to play expert golf. Thus, the drive to develop steel shafts. Lightweight steel gave manufacturers the ability to create hollow tubes of varying degrees of thickness. This led to an industry standard of five different flex ratings for golf shafts, indicated by a letter system: L (Ladies), A (Seniors), R (Regular), S (Stiff), and X (Extra Stiff).

Old hickory clubs had only one flex rating: a whole bunch. Bobby Jones used to lament the difficulty in finding a matched set of clubs because of the wide variation of flex. Problem solved. Well, not quite. There may have been an industry standard for designating flex but there was certainly no conformity from manufacturer to manufacturer on what a "regular flex" meant or what constituted a "stiff shaft." One company's off-the-shelf "R" might be the same as another's "A." Or worse. Independent tests have shown that clubs sold as Regular shafts can lie anywhere on the spectrum between L and X.

During a golf swing the shaft bends at a precise point somewhere along the arc, storing up energy. As the club straightens approaching impact that energy is released and club head speed is generated. At the 19th hole this is referred to as "loading and unloading the club." In general hard swingers who generate more than 100 miles per hour of clubhead speed are best served by stiffer shafts that throttle the flexing of the club. Golfers that rely on a smooth tempo need clubs that bend a little to produce extra distance - Regular shafts aimed at swing speeds between 90 and 100 miles per hour. A shafts are most effective for swing speeds between 80 and 90 miles per hour and L shafts for swing speeds below that.

Club fitters use a launch monitor to take measurements that uncover the ideal ball flight creating a bend profile of the club. This will reveal the ideal flex point for every golfer, that amount of flex that delivers the optimum accuracy, trajectory, and distance of every club right through the bag.

Shaft Weight

There is more to selecting the proper shaft than flex. The eternal struggle between "distance" and "feel" plays out in deciding on the ultimate weight of the shaft. Remember, the move away from steel towards graphite was predicated on weight - the lighter a golf shaft is, the faster the club can be swung and the more distance will be generated. Those weight savings can be applied to the clubhead or just used to produce an overall lightweight golf club.

The wizards that manufacturer graphite shafts can whittle the weight of a shaft below 50 grams. But the world's best players don't necessarily benefit from such a featherweight golf shaft. Most touring pros favor a shaft weight in the 60-75 gram range. Some prefer drivers with shafts that weigh up to 90 grams so as to "feel" the weight of the club in the swing. That feel is a key to building consistent moves in the golf swing that keep the club on plane going back and blasting down.

With the never-ending push for lighter and lighter shafts the natural assumption is that lighter is better. Faster is longer. Lighter is longer. Not quite so fast.

In golfspeak, lighter shafts produce a higher launch angle without giving up distance. In normal verbiage, lighter shafts make it easier to get the golf ball airborne. The most frustrating part of golf for beginners is to get the ball up in the air and moving down the fairway. But that may not be the case for every golfer. Finding an ideal shaft is an experimentation among ultralight, light and heavy shafts AND different flexes. Oh, and a few more things…

TMI-Torque, Flighting, Kickpoints...

Torque. When you poke your head down the rabbit hole of golf shafts there is more to see than just flex and shaft weight. You will also hear the word "torque." If you remember, the main thing wrong with those hickory shafts of yore was too much "torque" - twisting during the swing. These days that amount of twisting, actually the resistance to that twisting, is measured, albeit with no standard method. So you will see shafts with torque ratings in degrees, usually from 2 degrees to 6 degrees (the smaller the number, the more resistant to twisting in the swing).

What is the optimum amount of torque in a golf shaft? Who knows? Like finding the ideal flex and weight finding the perfect torque in a shaft is a personal mission of discovery. Touring pros usually swing away with low-torque clubs and recreational golfers find more use with shafts that torque more (3 or 4 degrees), producing a little more feel and clubhead speed.

Flighting. Flighting is a construction method that trims the tips of the shaft precisely so that the flex point is higher in the shorter scoring clubs and lower in the distance clubs. The concept is that this will promote a consistent ball flight through the bag. If you are starting to feel as if you, as a weekend golfer, were invited to the wrong party populated by gearheads and golf pros, just wait until the talk turns to kickpoints.

Kick-points. If you take a stick or something rod-like, like a golf shaft, and apply pressure on each end there will be a point where it bends. That is your kick-point. A golf shaft is tapered from the grip towards the clubhead and because of this configuration the club bends closer to the clubhead where there is less mass. If the kick-point is manipulated close to the tip it will encourage a higher ball launch and if the kick-point is higher on the shaft it will generate a lower ball flight.

You have seen there is a lot more going on with a golf shaft than simply connecting the grip to the clubhead. Much of the accepted wisdom involved with the golf shaft is based on science and the expected results are premised on a robot delivering the exact same perfect swing at the ball every time. The golfers selecting those shafts, however, are infested with swing flaws and personal preferences. It is up to the individual golfer to test different shafts and fine-tune the engine to the golf swing.

The Care and Feeding of Golf Shafts

You have your new shafts - congratulations. If they are steel, just a quick wipe after play will keep them looking sharp. If outfitted with rubber grips they can remain playable for several seasons with a regular scrubbing by a bristle brush and a dab of liquid hand soap. Never let your clubs sit in a bucket of water grip-end down during a cleaning session since moisture can accumulate from the butt end and cause unseen rust inside the grip. One day you will swing the club and be left holding only the grip as the snapped club cartwheels down the fairway.

Graphite shafts, on the other hand requires more attention. All those thousands of sensitive wound fibers are protected by a coat of polyurethane, much like enamel on a tooth. If the polyurethane wears off the only thing between the carbon fibers and the destructive forces of the outside world is a thin coat of paint that carries the silkscreen logo. If the paint is compromised the fibers are in danger of being cut or worn and the next step is a snapping of the shaft.

The best way to prevent this from happening is a quick monthly bath with water. No solvents or abrasive household cleaners that can rough up that critical polyurethane layer. When the shafts are dry you can apply a good furniture wax or even a specialty shaft wax that will keep your shafts gleaming factory-fresh for many seasons.

For caring for hickory shafts, woodworkers are known to be an individualistic lot, each with their favorite brews for the preservation of wood. To remove existing finishes a sanding with 60-grit paper and a light going over with 150-grit paper will do the job. A buffing with 0000 steel wool will ready the shaft for final finishing. That is the standard stuff.

Old time hickory golf club care manuals recommended linseed oil applications but original clubs now have wood aged maybe 100 years. Some woodworkers swear by shellac as the only go-to-finish for fine woods for its ease of application and ability to bring out deep, rich colors in the wood. Others turn to mixtures of oils that are sold commercially for gun stocks. Whatever you use, two coats are better than one.

Installing Your Own Golf Shafts

If you play golf long enough at some point you are going to be standing with the grip in one hand and the clubhead in the other - with parts of the shaft still inserted into each. Golf shops are happy to replace broken shafts but you can do it yourself with a hacksw, a heat gun and a workbench with a vise.

Step One

Begin by clearing the club head hosel of the broken shaft. Use the heat gun to break down the adhesive until it is possible to pull the shaft free. Turn up the heat gun for steel shafts, use patience and a lower heat setting for graphite shafts.

Step Two

Clean the inside of the hosel with a solvent until all adhesive is removed. Lifehack: mayonnaise can work the same magic as a commercial solvent.

Step Three

Prepare to cut your new shaft to the proper length by wrapping masking tape around the area where you plan to cut. With the hacksaw cut the new shaft to length.

Step Four

Rough up the tip of the shaft before inserting it into the hosel. This promotes adhesion. A sharp blade may be required to penetrate the protective polyurethane coating of graphite shafts.

Step Five

Special golf shaft epoxy will be required to make the permanent connection. Liberally cover the inside of the hosel with epoxy. If your club has a ferule (the small plastic ring at the top of the hosel) insert it at this point and also coat its interior with epoxy. Now slab the tip of the shaft with epoxy and push it the shaft into the hosel. Turn the shaft so it aligns properly to the club head - as John Wooden said, "Be quick, but don't hurry."

Step Six

Open the vise to remove the shaft. Check that it is fully inserted into the club head. Clean up any epoxy with solvent (or mayo) and set the club aside to dry overnight. All that is left is to attach the new grip.

Another title from Cruden Bay Books you may be interested in:

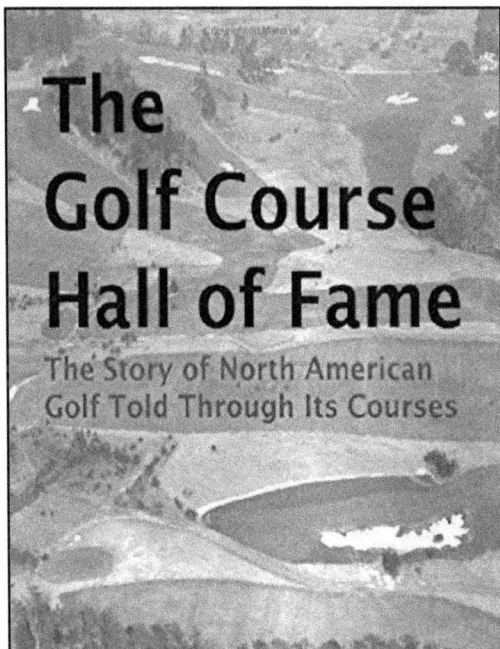

The Golf Course Hall of Fame

The Story of North American Golf Told Through Its Courses

There are 18,000 golf courses, more or less in some form or other, in North America. This is where the story of the game is written. It is a sprawling tale but a select few have contributed so mightily to the golf narrative of the past 125 years that they belong in a Hall of Fame. It is on theses courses that one finds not just the great champions, the great tournaments and the great architects but the story of senior golf...women's golf...televised golf...African American golf...retirement golf... miniature golf...collegiate golf... vacation golf...public golf...corporate golf...golf in the movies... nine-hole golf...Olympics golf...

Available now

184 pages   *$14.95*

www.golfcoursehalloffame.com

Since King Ludwig I of Bavaria introduced the concept of the Hall of Fame in the mid-19th century the herding together of immortals has become an American thing. There are an estimated 3,000 halls of fame for everything from hot dogs to pinball to mascots - but until now, not golf courses. Illustrated with over 170 historical photographs and fully indexed. No tee times required, just put it on the peg to get started.

You will want to discover...
- Who invented that golf tee? (page 13)
- What course spawned the mulligan? (page 101)
- What course had the first driving range? (page 55)
- What course pioneered the golf cart fleet? (page 110)
- What was considered the first million-dollar course to build? (page 124)
- What was the home course of the Three Stooges? (page 38)
- What course has a real bunker - intended for use by the federal government in the event of a nuclear attack? (page 79)
- Who was the model for the golfer atop the Ryder Cup? (page 34)
- What course inspired the Stimpmeter? (page 50)
- What course was named for near-sighted Harvard baseball players? (page 28)
- What course was Arnold Palmer playing when he met Winnie? (page 67)

www.ingramcontent.com/pod-product-compliance
Lightning Source LLC
Chambersburg PA
CBHW060648030426
42337CB00018B/3512